Early Praise for *Python Brain Teasers*

Miki Tebeka's brain teasers are a delightful and challenging collection of puzzles that will amuse novice Python developers and challenge experienced developers to think carefully about their mental model of Python execution.

Beyond amusement, the kind of thinking Miki urges on readers is genuinely important for all of us who have puzzled for far too long (and far too often) over some small snippet of code, written in our real codebases, that just "has to" do one thing, but actually does another.

➤ **Dr. David Mertz**
   Partner and Senior Trainer, KDM Training

Miki is a world-class Python and Go expert and a hands-on professional. This publication is another evidence that he comes from the field and that he can articulate not only the practical benefits and their practice but also the thought and the meta thinking behind them.

➤ **Shlomo Yona**
   Founder and Chief Scientist, mathematic.ai

I think even the seasoned Pythonista has a lot to learn from *Python Brain Teasers* by @tebeka.

➤ **David Bordeynik**
   Software Architect, NVIDIA

I strongly recommended this book to every Python programmer I know.

➤ **Mafinar Khan**
   Pythonista. Dartisan. Alchemist.

Python Brain Teasers

Exercise Your Mind

Miki Tebeka

The Pragmatic Bookshelf

Raleigh, North Carolina

Many of the designations used by manufacturers and sellers to distinguish their products are claimed as trademarks. Where those designations appear in this book, and The Pragmatic Programmers, LLC was aware of a trademark claim, the designations have been printed in initial capital letters or in all capitals. The Pragmatic Starter Kit, The Pragmatic Programmer, Pragmatic Programming, Pragmatic Bookshelf, PragProg and the linking *g* device are trademarks of The Pragmatic Programmers, LLC.

Every precaution was taken in the preparation of this book. However, the publisher assumes no responsibility for errors or omissions, or for damages that may result from the use of information (including program listings) contained herein.

For our complete catalog of hands-on, practical, and Pragmatic content for software developers, please visit *https://pragprog.com*.

The team that produced this book includes:

CEO: Dave Rankin
COO: Janet Furlow
Managing Editor: Tammy Coron
Development Editor: Margaret Eldridge
Copy Editor: Jennifer Whipple
Indexing: Potomac Indexing, LLC
Layout: Gilson Graphics
Founders: Andy Hunt and Dave Thomas

For sales, volume licensing, and support, please contact *support@pragprog.com*.

For international rights, please contact *rights@pragprog.com*.

ISBN-13: 978-1-68050-900-7
Book version: P1.0—September 2021

To the Python community, I'm proud to call myself a member.

Contents

Part I — Python Brain Teasers

Acknowledgments

I'm grateful for anyone who helped me write this book. Every contribution, from finding bugs to fixing grammar to letting me work in peace, was super helpful.

Here is a list of people who helped; my apologies to anyone I forgot:

- David Bordeynik for his comments and suggestions
- Elad Eyal for his comments
- Iddo Berger for his comments and suggestions
- Raymond Hettinger for lifelong Python education
- Shmuel Amar for his comments
- Yaki Tebeka for his comments
- Yehuda Lavy for his comments

Preface

The Python programming language is a simple one, but like all other languages it has its quirks. This book uses these quirks as a teaching opportunity. By understanding the gaps in your knowledge, you'll become better at what you do.

There's a lot of research showing that people who make mistakes during the learning process learn better than people who don't. If you use this approach when fixing bugs, you'll find you enjoy bug hunting more and become a better developer after each bug you fix.

These teasers will help you avoid mistakes. Some of the teasers are from my own experience shipping bugs to production, and some are from others doing the same.

Teasers are fun! We geeks love to solve puzzles. You can also use these teasers to impress your coworkers, have knowledge competitions, and become better together.

Many of these brain teasers are from quizzes I gave at conferences and meetups. I've found that people highly enjoy them and they tend to liven the room.

At the beginning of each chapter, I'll show you a short Python program and will ask you to guess the output. The following are the possible answers:

- Syntax error
- Exception
- Hang
- Some output (e.g., [1 2 3])

Python Version

 I'm using Python version 3.8.2 to run the code. The output *might* change in future versions.

Before moving on to the answer and the explanation, go ahead and guess the output. After guessing the output, I encourage you to run the code and see the output yourself; only then proceed to read the solution and the explanation. I've been teaching programming for many years and found this course of action to be highly effective.

About the Author

Miki Tebeka has a B.Sc. in computer science from Ben Gurion University. He also studied there toward an M.Sc. in computational linguistics.

Miki has a passion for teaching and mentoring. He teaches many workshops on various technical subjects all over the world and has mentored many young developers on their way to success. Miki is involved in open source, has several projects of his own, and has contributed to several more, including the Python project. He has been using Python for more than twenty-three years.

Miki wrote *Pandas Brain Teasers*, *Go Brain Teasers*, and *Forging Python* and is a LinkedIn Learning author and an organizer of Go Israel Meetup, GopherCon Israel, and PyData Israel Conference.

About the Code

You can find the brain teasers code at https://pragprog.com/titles/d-pybrain/python-brain-teasers/.

I've tried to keep the code as short as possible and remove anything that is not related to the teaser. This is *not* how you'll normally write code.

About You

I assume you know Python at some level and have experience programming with it. This book is not for learning how to program in Python. If you don't know Python, I'm afraid these brain teasers are not for you.

I recommend learning Python first (it's also fun). There are many resources online. Google is your friend.

One More Thing

As you work through the puzzles in this book, it might help to picture yourself as Nancy Drew, Sherlock Holmes, or any other of your favorite detectives trying to solve a murder mystery in which *you* are the murderer. Think of it like this:

> Debugging is like being a detective in a crime movie where you're also the murderer.
>
> — Filipe Fortes

With this mindset, I have found that things are easier to understand, and the work is more enjoyable. So, with that in mind, have fun guessing the brain teasers in this book—perhaps you might even learn a new trick or two.

If you'd like to learn more, please send an email to info@353solutions.com, and we'll tailor a hands-on workshop to meet your needs. There's also a comprehensive offering of hands-on workshops at www.353solutions.com.

Stay curious, and keep hacking!

Miki Tebeka, March 2020

Foreword by Raymond Hettinger

In my Python conference talks, I frequently check in with the audience to ask, "Have you learned something new?" Getting a "yes" over and over again fills everyone with delight and tells us that our time is being well-spent. Miki's collection of brain teasers will give you that immediate gratification, once per puzzle. Expect to have a lot fun with his stream of "aha!" moments.

Miki and I have worked together three times: once in a trading company, once at a web services company, and again as Python trainers. Working with him always gives you that "I learned something new" experience.

As trainers, we've found that a key skill is the ability to read code and to know, really know, what it does. With Miki's well-chosen examples, you can rapidly learn this essential skill. He gives you an interesting code fragment, asks you to make a prediction, and then gently explains the outcome. As icing on the cake, he also provides links to authoritative references to deepen your knowledge.

Python is not a difficult language, but there is much more to it than meets the eye. It is easy to assume you know the language well when you really don't. The Dunning-Kruger effect is pervasive in the Python world. Miki's brain teasers will help you quickly discover what you don't know, and his explanations will fill in the missing knowledge to build your expertise.

Here's an example that I've asked during interviews: What does this code do?

```python
for i in range(10):
    print(i)
    i = 5
print(i)
```

The answer quickly reveals whether someone understands iterators and scoping in Python. Miki's book is full of such gems.

Hope you enjoy the ride,
Raymond Hettinger
Python Core Developer with a PSF Distinguished Service Award

Part I

Python Brain Teasers

Ready Player One

```
player.py
class Player:
    # Number of players in the Game
    count = 0

    def __init__(self, name):
        self.name = name
        self.count += 1

p1 = Player('Parzival')
print(Player.count)
```

Guess the Output

 Try to guess what the output is before moving to the next page.

This code will print: 0

When you write self.count, you're doing an attribute lookup. The attribute you're looking for, in this case, is count.

Getting an attribute in Python is a complex operation. Almost every Python object stores its attributes in a dict called __dict__. Python will first try to find the attribute in the instance dictionary, then in the instance's class (__class__) dictionary, and then up the inheritance hierarchy (__mro__). Finally, if the attribute you're looking for is not found, Python will raise an AttributeError.

Attribute Lookup

 Python's attribute lookup is actually more complex than the previous explanation. Some objects such as C extensions and classes with __slots__ don't have a __dict__ and there are also descriptors, the __getattribute__ special methods, and other special cases.

Here's possible code for this algorithm, which is implemented in Python by the built-in getattr:

```python
def get_attr(obj, name):
    """Emulate built in getattr"""
    if name in obj.__dict__:
        print(f'found {name} in obj')
        return obj.__dict__[name]

    if name in obj.__class__.__dict__:
        print(f'found {name} in class')
        return obj.__class__.__dict__[name]

    for cls in obj.__class__.__mro__:
        if name in cls.__dict__:
            print(f'found {name} in {cls.__name__}')
            return cls.__dict__[name]

    raise AttributeError(name)
```

What happens when you do self.count += 1 in the teaser? Python will translate it to self.count = self.count + 1. Then it'll use getattr(self, count) and will get the count defined in Player with the value of 0. Once Python has the value of self.count + 1 = 1 on the right-hand side of the assignment (=), it'll call setattr(self, count, 1). setattr will create a new entry in self.__dict__ that will *shadow* the count in Player.

Lastly, you print Player.count, which is still 0. If you print p1.count you will get 1.

Further Reading

Class Instances
docs.python.org/3/reference/datamodel.html#index-49

Special Attributes
docs.python.org/3/library/stdtypes.html#special-attributes

Python's Class Development Toolkit (Video by Raymond Hettinger)
youtube.com/watch?v=HTLu2DFOdTg

Customizing Module Attribute Access
docs.python.org/3/reference/datamodel.html#customizing-module-attribute-access

Variable Shadowing on Wikipedia
en.wikipedia.org/wiki/Variable_shadowing

getattr Documentation
docs.python.org/3/library/functions.html#getattr

A Slice of π

pi.py
```
π = 355 / 113
print(π)
```

Guess the Output

 Try to guess what the output is before moving to the next page.

This code will print: 3.1415929203539825

There are two surprising things here: one is that π is a valid identifier, and the second is that 355 / 113 computes to a float.

Let's start with π (the Greek letter pi). Python 3 changed the default encoding for source files to UTF-8 and allows Unicode identifiers.

This can be fun to write, but in practice it'll make your coworkers' lives harder. I can easily type π in the Vim editor that I use; however, most editors and IDEs will require more effort.

One area where I've found that Unicode identifiers are helpful is when translating mathematical formulas to code. Apart from that, stick to plain old ASCII.

Now for 355 / 113. Python 3 does the right mathematical division. If you try this code in Python 2, you'll get 3 since Python 2 shows more of its C origins. If you want integer division to return an int in Python 3, use the // operator (e.g., 355 // 113). This is handy when calculating indices, which must be whole numbers.

Further Reading

Identifiers and Keywords in the Python Reference
docs.python.org/3/reference/lexical_analysis.html#identifiers

PEP 3120: Using UTF-8 as the Default Source Encoding
python.org/dev/peps/pep-3120/

PEP 263: Defining Python Source Code Encodings
python.org/dev/peps/pep-0263/

Vim Editor
vim.org

When in Kraków

```
city = 'Krako´w'
print(len(city))
```

Guess the Output

 Try to guess what the output is before moving to the next page.

This code will print: 7

Unicode

If you're reading this book in electronic format, don't copy and paste the code from the book; you'll probably get a different answer due to Unicode translation issues. Use the book source code. See the *About the Code* section on where to find it.

If you count the number of characters in Kraków, it'll come out to 6. So why 7? The reason is ... history.

In the beginning, computers were developed in English-speaking countries—the UK and the US. When early developers wanted to encode text in computers that only understand bits, they came out with the following scheme. Use a byte (8 bits) to represent a character. For example, a is 97 (01100001), b is 98, and so on. One byte is enough for the English alphabet, containing twenty-six lowercase letters, twenty-six uppercase letters, and ten digits. There is even some space left for other special characters (e.g., 9 for tab). This encoding is called ASCII. (To be precise, ASCII uses only 7 bits, and LATIN-1 extends it to 8 bits.)

After a while, other countries started to use computers and they wanted to write using their native languages. ASCII wasn't good enough; a single byte can't hold all the numbers needed to represent letters in different languages. This led to several different encoding schemes; the most common is UTF-8.

Some of the characters in UTF-8 are control characters. In this case we have the character o at position 4, and after it a control character saying "add an umlaut to the previous character." This is why the length of the string is 7.

In Python 3 you have str, which is an immutable sequence of Unicode code points, and bytes, which is an immutable sequence of bytes. At the edges of your program when you get bytes, convert it to a str using the decode method. When you send data, use the str.encode method to convert it to bytes. Internally, use str in your code.

Further Reading

Unicode HOWTO

    docs.python.org/3/howto/unicode.html

Unicode and You

    betterexplained.com/articles/unicode/

Unicode on Wikipedia
en.wikipedia.org/wiki/Unicode

"Pragmatic Unicode, or, How Do I Stop the Pain?" (Video)
youtube.com/watch?v=sgHbC6udIqc

ASCII on Wikipedia
en.wikipedia.org/wiki/ASCII

UTF-8 on Wikipedia
en.wikipedia.org/wiki/UTF-8

bytes.decode in the Python Documentation
docs.python.org/3/library/stdtypes.html#bytes.decode

str.encode in the Python Documentation
docs.python.org/3/library/stdtypes.html#str.encode

A Task to Do

tasks.py

Line 1
```
from heapq import heappush, heappop

tasks = []
heappush(tasks, (30, 'work out'))
heappush(tasks, (10, 'wake up'))
heappush(tasks, (20, 0xCAFFE))
heappush(tasks, (20, 'feed cat'))
heappush(tasks, (40, 'write book'))

while tasks:
    _, payload = heappop(tasks)
    print(payload)
```

Guess the Output

 Try to guess what the output is before moving to the next page.

This code will raise a TypeError exception.

The built-in heapq module implements min-heap over lists.

It's common to use a heap for a priority queue. Pushing and deleting from the heap are log(N) operations, and the first item in the heap (e.g., tasks[0]) is always the smallest.

To compare items in the heap, heapq uses the comparison defined in the object's type (using the < operator, which maps to the specific type's _lt_ special method). The objects in the tasks heap are tuples. Python orders tuples, and lists, in a lexicographical order, very much like books are ordered in the library. Lexicographical order compares the first two items, then the second two, and so on. Finally, if all of the items are equal, the longer tuple is considered bigger.

In line 11, you pop the first item from tasks, which is (10, 'wake up'). After this item is removed from the heap, heapq will move the smallest item to the top of the heap. There are two candidates (20, 'feed cat') and (20, 0xCAFFE); since the first items in these tuples are equal, Python will try to compare the second items.

l33t Code

 0xCAFFE is a hexadecimal (base 16) number. Writing "English" this way is called "leet" (or "l33t").

Comparing 'feed cat' (a str) with 0xCAFFE (an int) will raise an exception.

Further Reading

heapq Module
    docs.python.org/3/library/heapq.html

Heap Data Structure on Wikipedia
    en.wikipedia.org/wiki/Heap_(data_structure)

Lexicographical Order on Wikipedia
    en.wikipedia.org/wiki/Lexicographical_order

Tuples and Sequences
    docs.python.org/3/tutorial/datastructures.html#tuples-and-sequences

Send It to the Printer

printer.py

```
Line 1  from threading import Thread
        from time import sleep


     5  def printer():
            for i in range(3):
                print(i, end=' ')
                sleep(0.1)

    10
        thr = Thread(target=printer, daemon=True)
        thr.start()
        print()  # Add newline
```

Guess the Output

Try to guess what the output is before moving to the next page.

This code will print: 0

Output

Due to the unpredictable nature of threads, this code might not print anything.

In line 11, you start a daemon thread.

The Python documentation says

> The entire Python program exits when no alive non-daemon threads are left.

Since after the print() line there are no more non-daemon threads running, the process will exit. printer will manage to print the first number (0) and then the program will exit, taking down the thread with it.

If you see that your Python program finished working but seems to be "stuck," it's usually a sign there's a non-daemon thread running loose somewhere.

If you *do* want to wait for a thread to terminate, you can use the thread's join method.

```python
printer_join.py
from threading import Thread
from time import sleep


def printer():
    for i in range(3):
        print(i, end=' ')
        sleep(0.1)


thr = Thread(target=printer, daemon=True)
thr.start()
thr.join()
print()  # Add newline
```

Further Reading

Threading Module
docs.python.org/3/library/threading.html

Thread.join Documentation
docs.python.org/3/library/threading.html#threading.Thread.join

Spam, Spam, Spam

```
email.py
from email.message import EmailMessage

msg = EmailMessage()
msg['From'] = 'prince@palace.ng'
msg['To'] = 'Scrooge McDuck <scoorge@disney.com>'
msg.set_content('''\
Dear Sir.

I'm a Nigerian prince who came into some misfortune.
...
''')
print(msg)
```

Guess the Output

Try to guess what the output is before moving to the next page.

This code will raise a ModuleNotFoundError exception.

When Python looks for a module to import (e.g., email), it'll go over the directories in sys.path and try to find a module matching the name. The first value in sys.path is '' (the empty string). '' stands for the current directory, and in the current directory you have the teaser file email.py. Python will load this email.py instead of the one in the standard library and will not find the message submodule in it.

The lesson here: don't use module names already taken by the standard library. ☺

Python's import mechanism is pretty complex. Apart from .py files, it can import the following:

- Built-in modules (e.g., sys is "baked" into Python)
- Directories with _init_.py file in them
- Shared libraries (.so, .dll, .dyld ...)
- .pyc byte-compiled files (found in _pycache_ directory)
- And more

You can also add import hooks to import from other locations. There's a built-in hook to import from zip files and you can see python38.zip in sys.path.

To allow distributions to customize the import path, Python looks for site.py and loads it when it starts. You can run python -m site to view the import path.

If you'd like more freedom with package names, you can use relative imports. If you have a file called email.py in your package, it *can* import the system email. Inside your package you can use from .email import send_email to import the send_email from your package.

Further Reading

Import System
    docs.python.org/3/reference/import.html

importlib Module
    docs.python.org/3/library/importlib.html

"Modules and Packages: Live and Let Die!" Video by David Beazley
    youtube.com/watch?v=0oTh1CXRaQ0

Monty Python "Spam Song"
    youtube.com/watch?v=mBcY3W5WgNU

Relative Imports in the Python Documentation
    docs.python.org/3/reference/import.html#package-relative-imports

User! Identify Yourself

```
user.py
next_uid = 1

class User:
    def __init__(self, name):
        global next_uid

        self.name = name
        self.__id = next_uid
        next_uid += 1

u = User('daffy')
print(f'name={u.name}, id={u.__id}')
```

Guess the Output

 Try to guess what the output is before moving to the next page.

This code will raise an AttributeError exception.

Python does not have private and protected attributes like other languages (we joke that Python is a language for consenting adults).

By convention, if you prefix your attributes (or variables) with _ (called *underscore*), they are considered an implementation detail. You can still access them, but the author doesn't consider them part of the public API and might rename or remove them in the next version.

Say you choose to use _id in User. Now all the subclasses of User can't use their own _id attribute because they might run over the _id the methods in User use. The solution Python provides is called *name mangling*.

Let's have a look at the u's attributes.

```
>>> print(vars(u))  # Also print(u.__dict__)
{'name': 'daffy', '_User__id': 0}
```

_id was transformed into _User__id. Inside a User method, you can use _id and it'll work. But from "outside," including subclasses, this attribute is _User__id.

This approach frees the set of names classes can use for nonpublic attributes and methods. You can pick a name, add __ before it, and ensure no subclass will overrun it.

If someone really wants, they can still print(u._User__id) and it'll work. However, they are intentionally doing something risky.

Name mangling is not something unique to Python. It's also used in C, Java, and other languages. See the following links for more information.

Further Reading

Private Variables on the Python Documentation
   docs.python.org/3/tutorial/classes.html#private-variables

Name Mangling on Wikipedia
   en.wikipedia.org/wiki/Name_mangling

"Python's Class Development Toolkit" Video by Raymond Hettinger
   youtube.com/watch?v=HTLu2DFOdTg

sorted? reversed?

```
sorted.py
nums = [4, 1, 3, 2]
rev = reversed(nums)
print(sorted(rev) == sorted(rev))
```

Guess the Output

Try to guess what the output is before moving to the next page.

This code will print: False

The built-in reversed function returns an iterator.

Python's iterators can do two things:

- Return the next item (by using a for loop or calling the built-in next function)
- Signal there are no more items by raising StopIteration (we say the iterator is exhausted)

The first call to sorted(rev) consumes everything from the iterator. When you call sorted(rev) the second time, the iterator will immediately raise StopIteration and sorted will assume an empty iterator.

The result of the first sorted(rev) is [1, 2, 3, 4], and the result of the second sorted(rev) is [] (the empty list). This is why the comparison returns False.

Further Reading

reversed Documentation
    docs.python.org/3/library/functions.html#reversed

Iterator on "Functional Programming HOWTO"
    docs.python.org/3/howto/functional.html#functional-howto-iterators

Iterator on the Python Wiki
    wiki.python.org/moin/Iterator

"Generator Tricks for System Programmers" by David Beazley
    dabeaz.com/generators/

"Generators: The Final Frontier" Video by David Beazley
    youtube.com/watch?v=D1twn9kLmYg

itertools Module Code Examples
    docs.python.org/3/library/itertools.html

next Documentation
    docs.python.org/3/library/functions.html#next

A Simple Math

mul.py
```
print(1.1 * 1.1)
```

Guess the Output

 Try to guess what the output is before moving to the next page.

This code will print: 1.2100000000000002

You might have expected 1.21, which is the right mathematical answer.

Some new developers, when seeing this or similar output, come to the message boards and say, "We found a bug in Python!" The usual answer is, "Read the fine manual" (or RTFM for short).

> Floating point is sort of like quantum physics: the closer you look, the messier it gets.
>
> — Grant Edwards

The basic idea behind this issue is that floating points sacrifice accuracy for speed (i.e., cheat). Don't be shocked. It's a trade-off we do a lot in computer science.

The result you see conforms with the floating-point specification. If you run the same code in C, Java, Go ... you will see the same output.

See the links in the next section if you're interested in understanding more about how floating points work. The main thing you need to remember is that they are not accurate; and accuracy worsens as the number gets bigger.

One implication is that when testing involves floating points, you need to check for *roughly equal* and decide what is an acceptable threshold. The built-in unittest module has an assertAlmostEqual method for these cases. In the scientific Python world, numpy offers a versatile allclose function.

Floating points have several other oddities. For example, there's a special nan value (short for *not a number*). nan does not equal any number, *including itself.*

```
>>> float('nan') == float('nan')
False
```

To check that a value is nan, you need to use a special function such as math.isnan.

If you need better accuracy, look into the decimal module, which provides correctly rounded decimal floating-point arithmetic.

Further Reading

"Floating-Point Arithmetic: Issues and Limitations" in the Python Documentation
    docs.python.org/3/tutorial/floatingpoint.html

floating point zine by Julia Evans
    twitter.com/b0rk/status/986424989648936960

What Every Computer Scientist Should Know About Floating-Point Arithmetic
    docs.oracle.com/cd/E19957-01/806-3568/ncg_goldberg.html

IEEE 754 on Wikipedia
    en.wikipedia.org/wiki/IEEE_754

Built-in decimal Module
    docs.python.org/3/library/decimal.html

assertAlmostEqual Documentation
    docs.python.org/3/library/unittest.html#unittest.TestCase.assertAlmostEqual

numpy's allclose
    docs.scipy.org/doc/numpy/reference/generated/numpy.allclose.html

Will It Fit?

assign.py
```
a = [1, 2, 3, 4]
a[1:2] = [10, 20, 30]
print(a)
```

Guess the Output

 Try to guess what the output is before moving to the next page.

This code will print: [1, 10, 20, 30, 3, 4]

Python's slicing operator is half open ([) in math), meaning you'll get from the first index up to but not including the last index. a[1:2] is in size 1, yet we assign a list of size 3 to it.

The assignment documentation is a bit hard to read (see below if you're interested). Here's an excerpt (my clipping and emphasis):

> If the target is a slicing: ... Finally, the sequence object is asked to replace the slice with the items of the assigned sequence. *The length of the slice may be different from the length of the assigned sequence* ...

In short, when you write a[1:2] = [10, 20, 30] it's like writing a = a[:1] + [10, 20, 30] + a[2:].

Further Reading

Assignment Statements on the Python Reference
docs.python.org/3/reference/simple_stmts.html#assignment-statements

Informal Introduction to Python
docs.python.org/3/tutorial/introduction.html

Slice Type
docs.python.org/3/library/functions.html#slice

Python's List Type
docs.python.org/3/tutorial/datastructures.html#more-on-lists

Click the Button

```
buttons.py
Line 1  display = []
  2     buttons = []
  3     for n in range(10):
  4         # A button is a function called when user clicks on it
  5         buttons.append(lambda: display.append(n))
  6
  7     btn = buttons[3]
  8     btn()
  9     print(display)
```

Guess the Output

Try to guess what the output is before moving to the next page.

This code will print: [9]

You probably expected [3] since each lambda appends its n to display.

However, the n that each lambda uses is the same n defined in line 3. This type of variable binding is known as a *closure*.

You have two options to fix this bug. The first, and my preference, is to have a make_button(n) function.

buttons_make.py
```
display = []
buttons = []

def make_button(n):
    return lambda: display.append(n)

for n in range(10):
    # A button is a function called when user clicks on it
    buttons.append(make_button(n))
btn = buttons[3]
btn()
print(display)
```

The second solution is to use the fact that default function arguments are evaluated once at function creation.

buttons_default.py
```
display = []
buttons = []
for n in range(10):
    # A button is a function called when user clicks on it
    buttons.append(lambda n=n: display.append(n))  # <1>
btn = buttons[3]
btn()
print(display)
```

The n=n defines a function parameter that shadows the n from the outer scope.

Further Reading

PEP 227: Statically Nested Scopes
    python.org/dev/peps/pep-0227/

PEP 3104: Access to Names in Outer Scopes
    python.org/dev/peps/pep-3104/

Closure on Wikipedia
en.wikipedia.org/wiki/Closure_(computer_programming)

Variable Shadowing on Wikipedia
en.wikipedia.org/wiki/Variable_shadowing

Attention Seeker

```
seeker.py
Line 1  class Seeker:
     2      def __getattribute__(self, name):
     3          if name not in self.__dict__:
     4              return '<not found>'
     5          return self.__dict__[name]
     6
     7
     8  s = Seeker()
     9  print(s.id)
```

Guess the Output

Try to guess what the output is before moving to the next page.

This code will raise a RecursionError exception.

When you write s.id, Python does an attribute lookup (see puzzle 1, *Ready Player One*). Python defines several hooks to bypass the usual attribute lookup algorithm. The two main options are _getattr_ and _getattribute_.

Other Options

 There are several other ways to modify attribute access such as staticmethod, classmethod, properties, descriptors, and more.

getattr is called when the regular attribute lookup fails, and it's usually the one you should use. _getattribute_ bypasses the attribute lookup and gives you full control.

> With great power comes great responsibility.
>
> — Uncle Ben

Since _getattribute_ bypasses the attribute lookup, the code self._dict_ in line 3 will call _getattribute_ again, and you descend into infinite recursion. Python has a guard against infinite recursions. Once the call stack size is more than sys.getrecursionlimit() a RecursionError will be raised. That is what you see in this teaser.

You can increase the recursion limit with sys.setrecursionlimt. Unless you have a really good reason, don't do that.

Dictionaries in Python provide a similar hook to _getattr_ called _missing_. You can implement collections.defaultdict and the like with _missing_.

Further Reading

Class Instances
docs.python.org/3/reference/datamodel.html#index-49

"Customizing Attribute Access" on the Python Reference
docs.python.org/3/reference/datamodel.html#customizing-attribute-access

"Descriptor HowTo Guide" on the Python Documentation
docs.python.org/3/howto/descriptor.html

getattr Documentation
docs.python.org/3/reference/datamodel.html#object._getattr_

getattribute Documentation

    docs.python.org/3/reference/datamodel.html#object.__getattribute__)

missing Documentation

    docs.python.org/3/reference/datamodel.html#object.__missing__

collections.defaultdict Documentation

    docs.python.org/3/library/collections.html#collections.defaultdict

Identity Crisis

identity.py

```
a, b = 12, 3
x = a * b
y = b * a
print(x is y)
```

Guess the Output

Try to guess what the output is before moving to the next page.

This code will print: True

A Python variable is a name pointing to a Python object. When you have two variables (such as x and y), you can ask two questions:

Equality
 Are the objects these variables point to equal? (the == operator)

Identity
 Do these two variables point to the same object? (the is operator)

Since you did two separate calculations for x and y, you'd expect them to be equal but not identical. In general, you'd be right. Change the value of b to 333 and re-run; you will see False as the output.

The reason you're seeing True is due to an implementation detail. Since the small numbers are used a lot, Python is *interning* them.

Here's what the documentation says:

> The current implementation keeps an array of integer objects for all integers between -5 and 256; when you create an int in that range you actually just get back a reference to the existing object.

Meaning there's only one copy of the number 1 in a Python program. Every calculation that results in 1 returns the same object.

Further Reading

PyLong_FromLong Documentation
 docs.python.org/3/c-api/long.html#c.PyLong_FromLong

String Interning on Wikipedia
 en.wikipedia.org/wiki/String_interning

Flyweight Pattern on Wikipedia
 en.wikipedia.org/wiki/Flyweight_pattern

The Great Divide

```
div.py
def div(a, b):
    return a / b

if div(1, 2) > 0 or div(1, 0) > 0:
    print('OK')
else:
    print('oopsie')
```

Guess the Output

 Try to guess what the output is before moving to the next page.

This code will print: OK

You probably expected this code to raise ZeroDivisionErro due to div(1, 0).

If you call div(1, 0) by itself, you will see the exception. Yet the logic operators in Python, and and or, are short-circuit operators.

Here's what the documentation says on and:

> This is a short-circuit operator, so it only evaluates the second argument if the first one is false.

In contrast, all arguments to a function call are evaluated before calling the function. This means you can't write your own my_and function that will behave like the built-in and.

You can use this to your advantage. Say you'd like to load the current user from the database (slow operation) only if the user is not in the session.

```
user = session.get('user') or load_current_user()
```

load_current_user() will be called only if session.get('user') returns None (which is False in Python).

If you write

```
user = session.get('user', load_current_user())
```

then load_current_user() will be called *every time*, even if the user is in the session.

Further Reading

"Boolean Operations—and, or, not" in the Python Documentation
    docs.python.org/3/library/stdtypes.html#boolean-operations-and-or-not

Short-Circuit Evaluation on Wikipedia
    en.wikipedia.org/wiki/Short-circuit_evaluation

Where's Waldo?

waldo.py
```python
name = 'Waldo'
text = 'Can you find where Wally is?'

if text.find(name):
    print('Found Waldo')
else:
    print('Cannot find Waldo')
```

Guess the Output

Try to guess what the output is before moving to the next page.

This code will print: Found Waldo

The str.find documentation says

> Return -1 if sub is not found.

We have two Boolean values in Python: True and False. They weren't always there; they were added in Python 2.3.

How can you do logical operations without True and False? There are *rules*! Everything is True except

- 0 numbers: 0, 0.0, 0+0j, ...
- Empty collections: [], {}, '', ...
- None
- False

You can test the truth value of a Python object using the built-in bool function.

Going back to the teaser, text.find(name) returns -1, and the Boolean value of -1 is True.

If you want to check whether a string contains another, use the in operator:

```
if name in text:
    print('Found Waldo')
else:
    print('Cannot find Waldo')
```

This will print Cannot find Waldo.

If you want to define a Boolean logic for your object, implement the __bool__ special method.

Further Reading

str.find Documentation
docs.python.org/3/library/stdtypes.html#str.find

PEP 285: Adding a bool Type
python.org/dev/peps/pep-0285/

"Truth Value Testing" in the Python Documentation
docs.python.org/3/library/stdtypes.html#truth-value-testing

__bool__ Documentation
docs.python.org/3/reference/datamodel.html#object.__bool__

Call Me Maybe

metrics.py

```
from functools import wraps

def metrics(fn):
    ncalls = 0
    name = fn.__name__

    @wraps(fn)
    def wrapper(*args, **kw):
        ncalls += 1
        print(f'{name} called {ncalls} times')

    return wrapper

@metrics
def inc(n):
    return n + 1

inc(3)
```

Guess the Output

 Try to guess what the output is before moving to the next page.

This code will raise an UnboundLocalError exception.

When you have a variable (name) in Python (say, cart = ['lamp']), you can do two operations:

Mutate

Change the object the variable is pointing to (e.g., cart.append('mug'))

Rebind

Have the variable point to another object (e.g., cart = ['carrots'])

When you mutate, the variable can be in any scope. However, when you rebind a variable, you need to be in the same scope as the variable.

What are these *scopes*? It's where the name you're using currently is defined. Let's see an example:

```
scale = 1.1

def make_mul(n):
    def mul(val):
        out = val * n * scale
        return out
    return mul

mul7 = make_mul(7)
print(mul7(3))  # 23.1
```

- val is local scope, n is enclosing scope, scale is global scope.
- out is from local scope.

When Python sees a name (e.g., ncalls), it looks for it in LEGB order:

- Local
- Enclosing (closure)
- Global
- Builtin

Builtin refers to the builtins module.

Abusing the builtins Module

 If you want to define something that can be accessed from *any* module, you can stick it in builtins. Don't do that. ☺

Since integers are immutable in Python, the += operator rebinds the variable on the left side of it to a new integer object. Since ncalls is from the enclosing scope, you can't rebind it without being more specific.

Python 2 has the global keyword for rebinding global variables, and Python 3 added the nonlocal keyword for rebinding enclosing variables. You can use nonlocal in this teaser.

metrics_nl.py

```
from functools import wraps

def metrics(fn):
    ncalls = 0
    name = fn.__name__

    @wraps(fn)
    def wrapper(*args, **kw):
        nonlocal ncalls
        ncalls += 1
        print(f'{name} called {ncalls} times')

    return wrapper

@metrics
def inc(n):
    return n + 1

inc(3)
```

If you're in Python 2, you do the following trick (called *boxing*).

metrics_box.py

```
Line 1  from functools import wraps


        def metrics(fn):
     5      ncalls = [0]
            name = fn.__name__

            @wraps(fn)
            def wrapper(*args, **kw):
    10          ncalls[0] += 1
                print(f'{name} called {ncalls[0]} times')

            return wrapper

    15
        @metrics
        def inc(n):
            return n + 1

    20
        inc(3)
```

Now, in line 10, you're not rebinding ncalls; you're mutating it and that is OK.

Further Reading

Assignment Statements in the Python Documentation
docs.python.org/3/reference/simple_stmts.html#assignment-statements

PEP 227: Statically Nested Scopes
python.org/dev/peps/pep-0227/

Nonlocal Statement in the Python Documentation
docs.python.org/3/reference/simple_stmts.html#nonlocal

Global Statement in the Python Documentation
docs.python.org/3/reference/simple_stmts.html#global

"What Are the Rules for Local and Global Variables in Python?" in the Python FAQ
docs.python.org/3/faq/programming.html#what-are-the-rules-for-local-and-global-variables-in-python

"Why Am I Getting an UnboundLocalError When the Variable Has a Value?" in the Python FAQ
docs.python.org/3/faq/programming.html#why-am-i-getting-an-unboundlocalerror-when-the-variable-has-a-value

builtins Module
docs.python.org/3/library/builtins.html#module-builtins

Endgame

avengers.py

```
Line 1  avengers = ['Bruce', 'Carol', 'Natasha', 'Tony']
   2  idx = 3
   3  avengers[idx], idx = 'Peter', 2
   4  print(avengers)
```

Guess the Output

 Try to guess what the output is before moving to the next page.

This code will print: ['Bruce', 'Carol', 'Natasha', 'Peter']

You're doing multiple assignments, also known as *unpacking*. In line 3, Python will first evaluate the right side of the = from left to right and then assign to the left side, again from left to right.

In the line avengers[idx], idx = 'Peter', 2, Python first evaluates avengers[idx] = 'Peter'. Since idx is still 3 here, the fourth item on the list, Tony, is being replaced. Then Python will evaluate idx = 2.

This is confusing and considered bad practice. Don't do it.

Further Reading

PEP 3132: Extended Iterable Unpacking
   python.org/dev/peps/pep-3132/

PEP 448: Additional Unpacking Generalizations
   python.org/dev/peps/pep-0448/

Evaluation Order in the Python Reference
   docs.python.org/3/reference/expressions.html#evaluation-order

Round and Round We Go

round.py
```
print(round(1.5), round(2.5))
```

Guess the Output

 Try to guess what the output is before moving to the next page.

This code will print: 2 2

Rounding seems easy. round(1.1) evaluates to 1. round(1.8) evaluates to 2. The question is, how do you round the .5 numbers? Should you round up? Down? Turns out, there are a lot of ways to do it.

Python 3 uses *bankers' rounding*. Odd numbers are rounded up; even numbers are rounded down. The reasoning behind this method is that if you round a list of numbers, assuming there's roughly the same number of odd and even numbers, the error (rounding) will cancel each other.

Python 2 uses a different method called *round away from zero*. If you run this teaser in Python 2, you'll see (2.0, 3.0) as the output.

Further Reading

Rounding on Wikipedia
>   en.wikipedia.org/wiki/Rounding

Built-in round Documentation
>   docs.python.org/3/library/functions.html#round

Floating-Point Arithmetic: Issues and Limitations in the Python Tutorial
>   docs.python.org/3/tutorial/floatingpoint.html#tut-fp-issues

TF (Without IDF)

```
word_freq.py
Line 1  import re
        from collections import defaultdict


     5  def word_freq(text, freqs=defaultdict(int)):
            """Calculate word frequency in text. freqs are previous frequencies"""
            for word in [w.lower() for w in re.findall(r'\w+', text)]:
                freqs[word] += 1
            return freqs
    10

        freqs1 = word_freq('Duck season. Duck!')
        freqs2 = word_freq('Rabbit season. Rabbit!')
        print(freqs1)
    15  print(freqs2)
```

Guess the Output

Try to guess what the output is before moving to the next page.

This code will print:

```
defaultdict(<class 'int'>, {'duck': 2, 'season': 2, 'rabbit': 2})
defaultdict(<class 'int'>, {'duck': 2, 'season': 2, 'rabbit': 2})
```

One of the solutions to the *Click the Button* puzzle is using the fact that default arguments to a function are evaluated once when the function is defined. Here you see the dark side of this aspect.

Mutable default arguments are considered bad practice, and linters such as flake8 or pylint will mark line 5 in this teaser code as an error.

The solution is to use `None` as the default value and in the function itself to create the mutable default.

word_freq_none.py
```
import re
from collections import import defaultdict


def word_freq(text, freqs=None):
    """Calculate word frequency in text. freqs are previous frequencies"""
    freqs = defaultdict(int) if freqs is None else freqs
    for word in [w.lower() for w in re.findall(r'\w+', text)]:
        freqs[word] += 1
    return freqs


freqs1 = word_freq('Duck season. Duck!')
freqs2 = word_freq('Rabbit season. Rabbit!')
print(freqs1)
print(freqs2)
```

Further Reading

flake8 Linter
> flake8.pycqa.org

pylint Linter
> pylint.org

Default Argument Values in the Python Tutorial
> docs.python.org/3/tutorial/controlflow.html#default-argument-values

Common Gotchas in the "Hitchhiker's Guide to Python"
> docs.python-guide.org/writing/gotchas/

tf-idf on Wikipedia
> en.wikipedia.org/wiki/Tf%E2%80%93idf

A Divided Time

```
Line 1  class timer:
            def __init__(self, name):
                self.name = name

     5      def __enter__(self):
                ...

            def __exit__(self, exc_type, exc_value, traceback):
                result = 'OK' if exc_type is None else 'ERROR'
    10          print(f'{self.name} - {result}')
                return True


        with timer('div'):
    15      1 / 0
```

Guess the Output

Try to guess what the output is before moving to the next page.

This code will print: div - ERROR

You might have expected to see a ZeroDivisionError exception.

timer is a context manager. A context manager is used with the with statement and is usually for managing resources. For example, with open('input.txt') will make sure that the file is closed after the code inside the context manager is done, even if the code inside the with raised an exception.

There are several types in the Python standard library that can be used with a with statement:

- A file will be closed.
- A socket will be closed.
- A threading.Lock will be released.

There's one resource you don't need to explicitly manage: the memory. Python has a garbage collector that manages the memory for you.

All other resources need to be managed manually. For example, if you forget to close a file, you will reach the operating system limit on the number of open files. Your server will start failing after a while with too many open files errors.

Some database packages also support with statements but with different semantics. If there's no error, they will issue a COMMIT; otherwise, they will issue a ROLLBACK.

You can implement context managers either by writing a class with _enter_ and _exit_ methods (like we do in the teaser) or by using the contextlib.contextmanager decorator.

The _exit_ method is called when the code inside the with statement is done, and its arguments will be None if there was no exception. If _exit_ returns a False value, the exception will propagate; otherwise, the exception is suppressed.

Most _exit_ methods don't return a value, which in Python means it returns None, whose Boolean value is False.

In the teaser, _exit_ returns True, suppressing the ZeroDivisionError.

Oh, and the ... in line 6 is called *ellipsis*; it's valid Python.

Further Reading

Context Manager Types in the Python Documentation
docs.python.org/3/library/stdtypes.html#typecontextmanager

PEP 343: The "with" Statement
python.org/dev/peps/pep-0343/

contextlib Module
docs.python.org/3/library/contextlib.html

Commit on Wikipedia
en.wikipedia.org/wiki/Commit_(data_management)

Rollback on Wikipedia
en.wikipedia.org/wiki/Rollback_(data_management)

Ellipsis on the Python Documentation
docs.python.org/3/library/constants.html#Ellipsis

Tell Me the Future

future.py

```python
from datetime import datetime

date = datetime(10_000, 1, 1)
print(f'The party started on {date:%B, %d %Y} and lasted a 10 days')
```

Guess the Output

Try to guess what the output is before moving to the next page.

This code will raise a ValueError.

Computers and time have a complicated relationship. There are daylight saving time, leap years, time zones, and more details to work out.

Computers store time as the number of seconds that elapsed since January 1, 1970, GMT, known as Unix or epoch time. This means that in 2038, time will overflow on 32-bit machines. Ouch!

Python has two libraries to work with time:

- The good old time module
- The new and shiny datetime module

This teaser uses datetime, which is written mostly in C and has a fixed amount of space for storing time information. This means there's a maximal and minimal value to datetime.

```
>>> from datetime import datetime
>>> print(datetime.min, datetime.max)
0001-01-01 00:00:00 9999-12-31 23:59:59.999999
```

The value provided in the teaser is bigger than the maximal value for datetime, hence, the ValueError exception.

Further Reading

time Module Documentation
   docs.python.org/3/library/time.html

datetime Module Documentation
   docs.python.org/3/library/datetime.html

Falsehoods Programmers Believe About Time
   infiniteundo.com/post/25326999628/falsehoods-programmers-believe-about-time

Unix Time on Wikipedia
   en.wikipedia.org/wiki/Unix_time

Year 2038 Problem on Wikipedia
   en.wikipedia.org/wiki/Year_2038_problem

Loop de Loop

loop.py
```
for n in range(5):
    print(n, end=' ')
    n = 5
print()
```

Guess the Output

 Try to guess what the output is before moving to the next page.

This code will print: 0 1 2 3 4

Python's for loop is a "for each." Iteration in Python involves two types:

Iterable

> The object we're iterating over (e.g., str, list, dict ...)

Iterator

> Does the actual iteration; can *only* fetch the next item and signal it's done (i.e., exhausted) by raising a StopIteration

Here's what the for loop looks like under the hood.

```
loop_internal.py
iterable = range(5)  # range is the iterable
iterator = iter(iterable)  # extract iterator from iterable
while True:
    try:
        n = next(iterator)
        # Code inside "for" loop
        print(n, end=' ')
        n = 5  # Will be overridden by line 5 in next iteration
    except StopIteration:  # iterator signaled it's exhausted
        break
print()  # Code after "for" loop
```

From this code, it's clear why n = 5 will not stop the for loop.

You can create iterators for your own type by creating a class that implements two methods: _next_ and _iter_. Your iterable type should implement _iter_ that returns the iterator.

Or ... you can choose the easier path and implement a generator.

Further Reading

next Documentation

> docs.python.org/3/library/stdtypes.html#iterator._next_

iter Documentation

> docs.python.org/3/library/stdtypes.html#iterator._iter_

Iterator Types in the Python Documentation

> docs.python.org/3/library/stdtypes.html#iterator-types

Generators on the Python Wiki

> wiki.python.org/moin/Generators

"Generator Tricks for System Programmers" by David Beazley
dabeaz.com/generators/

itertools Module Code Examples
docs.python.org/3/library/itertools.html

Path to Nowhere

winpath.py
```
path = 'c:\path\to\nowhere'
print(path)
```

Guess the Output

Try to guess what the output is before moving to the next page.

This code will print:

```
c:\path o
owhere
```

The \ in Python strings is used as an escape sequence to write special characters. \t translates to the tab character, and \n translates to the newline character.

There are several other ways you can escape special characters in strings.

```
escape.py
s1 = '\x61'  # \x - 2 digits
print(s1)  # a

s2 = '\u2122'  # \u - 4 digits (8482 in hex)
print(s2)  # ™

s3 = '\U00002122'  # \U - 8 digits
print(s3)  # ™

s4 = '\N{trade mark sign}'
print(s4)  # ™
```

What if you want a \ inside your string? You can escape it with another \.

```
path = 'c:\\path\\to\\nowhere'
```

The easier approach is to use a *raw* string. Here's what the documentation says:

> Both string and bytes literals may optionally be prefixed with a letter 'r' or 'R'; such strings are called raw strings and treat backslashes as literal characters.

In this case

```
path = r'c:\path\to\nowhere'
```

The two most common use cases for raw strings are Windows paths (when you cut and paste from Explorer) and when defining regular expressions that have special characters that start with \ (e.g., \s for white space).

Further Reading

String and Bytes Literals in the Python Reference
    docs.python.org/3/reference/lexical_analysis.html#string-and-bytes-literals

Find Fun Unicode Characters in the Unicode Table
    unicode-table.com/en/

Regular Expression Syntax in the Python Documentation
    docs.python.org/3/library/re.html#regular-expression-syntax

12 Angry Men

jury.py
```python
from concurrent.futures import ProcessPoolExecutor
from itertools import repeat

guilty = 0

def juror():
    global guilty

    guilty += 1

with ProcessPoolExecutor() as pool:
    for _ in repeat(None, 12):
        pool.submit(juror)

print(guilty)
```

Guess the Output

 Try to guess what the output is before moving to the next page.

This code will print: 0

Both threads and processes are concurrent units of work. The main difference is that threads share the same memory space and processes don't.

This means that if you have a global variable (e.g., guilty), all threads in the same process will be able to access and modify it. Whereas in processes, you will need to communicate the data between the processes in some way (e.g., a socket).

This teaser uses a ProcessPoolExecutor, meaning the code is executed in a different process. Every juror changes its own copy of guilty.

Threads allow faster access to shared data, but they are more dangerous. None of the built-in types in Python (e.g., list, dict, ...) are thread safe. If you change (i.e., mutate) a list from two threads at the same time, the behavior is undefined. You'll need to use threading.Lock to guard that only one thread changes the list at a time.

Making all built-in types thread-safe will make them much slower, and most of the Python code out there still runs in a single thread. This is why the built-in types will not be thread-safe in the near (or far) future.

When should you use threads and when processes? The rule of thumb is that if you have CPU-bound code, you should use processes, and if you have an I/O-bound code you should use threads.

Before moving to threads or processes, remember that there's a limit on how much parallelization will help you and that it's much harder to write such code than sequential code.

Further Reading

concurrent.futures Module
> docs.python.org/3/library/concurrent.futures.html

Amdahl's Law on Wikipedia
> en.wikipedia.org/wiki/Amdahl%27s_law

I/O-bound on Wikipedia
> en.wikipedia.org/wiki/I/O_bound

CPU-bound on Wikipedia
> en.wikipedia.org/wiki/CPU-bound

Lock in the Python Documentation
docs.python.org/3/library/threading.html#lock-objects

"Using repeat Over range" by Raymond Hettinger
twitter.com/raymondh/status/1144527183341375488?lang=en

Look at the Pretty Colors

colors.py
```
colors = [
    'red',
    'green'
    'blue'
]

print(colors)
```

Guess the Output

 Try to guess what the output is before moving to the next page.

This code will print: ['red', 'greenblue']

Python's use of white space is pretty unique in programming languages. Some people don't like it. I personally find it makes the code more readable.

The Python documentation says

> A logical line is constructed from one or more physical lines by following the explicit or implicit line joining rules.

And a bit later

> Expressions in parentheses, square brackets, or curly braces can be split over more than one physical line without using backslashes.

Which means

- 'a' 'b' is not valid.
- ('a', 'b') is a tuple ('a', 'b' is also a tuple).
- ('a' 'b') is the string 'ab'.

In the teaser, there is a , missing between 'green' and 'blue'. Python will join them together as 'greenblue'.

This is why you should have a *dangling comma* when you write expressions like colors:

```
colors = [
    'red',
    'green',
    'blue',  # ← A dangling comma
]
```

Not only will it save you from bugs, in code reviews, if you add another color, there will be only one line change. Sadly, not every language or format allows dangling commas. I'm looking at you JSON and SQL.

---

black

 You can use the black code formatter with your IDE. It will format your code and add dangling commas.

You can use this *implicit line joining* to make your code clearer. Here's an example from the matplotlib documentation:

Turn

```
plot(x, y, color='green', marker='o', linestyle='dashed', linewidth=2, markersize=12)
```

into

```
plot(
        x, y,
        color='green',
        marker='o', markersize=12,
        linestyle='dashed', linewidth=2,
)
```

You can even surround your code with () and do *method chaining*:

```
(
        df[df['passenger_count'] > 1]  # rides with more than 1
        ['tpep_pickup_datetime'].dt.hour  # extract hour
        .value_counts()  # count hours
        .sort_index()  # sort by hour
        .plot.bar(rot=45, title='11am rides')  # plot with 45° axis labels
)
```

Further Reading

Line Structure in the Python Reference
   docs.python.org/3/reference/lexical_analysis.html#line-structure

When to Use Trailing Commas in the "Style Guide for Python" (aka PEP 8)
   python.org/dev/peps/pep-0008/#id29

Tuple Syntax on the Python Wiki
   wiki.python.org/moin/TupleSyntax

"That Trailing Comma" by Dave Cheney
   dave.cheney.net/2014/10/04/that-trailing-comma

Matplotlib Documentation
   matplotlib.org

Black Code Formatter
   black.readthedocs.io

Let's Vote

vote.py
```python
import re

text = 'The vote was 65 in favour, 43 against and 21 abstentions'
match = re.search(r'(\d+).*(\d+).*(\d+)', text)
print(match.group(1), match.group(2), match.group(3))
```

Guess the Output

Try to guess what the output is before moving to the next page.

This code will print: 65 2 1

You might have expected to see 65 43 21. The reason for this output is that the .* regular expression is *greedy*, which means it will match as much as it can. Here's what happened:

- The first .*(\d+) will match 65.
- The .* after it will match in favour, 43 against and.
- The next .*(\d+) will match 2.
- The .* after it will match the empty string since * means *zero or more*.
- The final .*(\d+) will match 1.

To make .* nongreedy, add ? at the end. The following will work as expected:

```
match = re.search(r'(\d+).*?(\d+).*?(\d+)', text)
```

You can use sites such as www.pyregex.com/ to test your regular expressions.

Further Reading

re Module
    docs.python.org/3/library/re.html

"Regular Expression HOWTO" in the Python Documentation
    docs.python.org/3/howto/regex.html

An Inside Job

```
inside.py
def add_n(items, n):
    items += range(n)

items = [1]
add_n(items, 3)
print(items)
```

Guess the Output

 Try to guess what the output is before moving to the next page.

This code will print: [1, 0, 1, 2]

In the *Call Me Maybe* puzzle, we talked about rebinding versus mutation. And most of the time, items += range(n) is translated to items = items + range(n), which is rebinding.

There is a special optimization for += in some cases. Here's what the documentation says (my emphasis):

> An augmented assignment expression like x += 1 can be rewritten as x = x + 1 to achieve a similar, but not exactly equal, effect. In the augmented version, x is only evaluated once. Also, *when possible, the actual operation is performed in place, meaning that rather than creating a new object and assigning that to the target, the old object is modified instead.*

A type defines how the + operator behaves with the _add_ special method and can define _iadd_ as a special case for +=. The documentation says

> These methods are called to implement the augmented arithmetic assignments (+=, -=, =, @=, /=, //=, %=, *=, <=, >>=, &=, ^=, |=). These methods should attempt to do the operation in place (modifying self) and return the result (which could be, but does not have to be, self). If a specific method is not defined, the augmented assignment falls back to the normal methods.

The built-in list object defines _iadd_, which calls the extend method.

What will happen if you change the code inside add_n to items = items + range(n)? You will get an exception: TypeError: can only concatenate list (not "range") to list.

In Python 3 the built-in range function returns a range object. Even though it *looks* like a list (len, [], and friends will work), you can't add it to a list.

If you want the rebinding code to work, you'll need to write items = items + list(range(n)) and then the output will be [1].

As a general rule, try not to mutate the object passed to your functions. This style of programming is called *functional* programming. Functional code is easier to test and reason about. Give it a try. It's fun.

Further Reading

Functional Programming on Wikipedia
en.wikipedia.org/wiki/Functional_programming

Built-in range Documentation
docs.python.org/3/library/functions.html#func-range

"Augmented Assignment Statements" in the Python Reference
    docs.python.org/3/reference/simple_stmts.html#augmented-assignment-statements

"Functional Programming HOWTO" in the Python Documentation
    docs.python.org/3/howto/functional.html

__iadd__ Documentation
    docs.python.org/3/reference/datamodel.html#object.__iadd__

"More on Lists" in the Python Documentation
    docs.python.org/3/tutorial/datastructures.html#more-on-lists

Here Kitty Kitty

cat.py

```
pali = 'Was it a cat I saw?'
print(pali[::-1])
```

Guess the Output

 Try to guess what the output is before moving to the next page.

This code will print: ?was I tac a ti saW

Palindrome

"Was it a cat I saw?" is a palindrome. A palindrome can be read the same backward and forward.

And no, Officer Ripley, it wasn't a cat you saw. ☺

This is the best way to reverse a string in Python:

pali[::-1] is a string slice. Slices have start, stop, and step, each of them optional. start to stop is a *half-open* range, meaning you'll get from the first index up to but not including the last. Additionally, if you specify a negative stop, it'll be an offset from the end.

Let's see some examples:

```
>>> 'Python'[1:4]  # start & stop
'yth'
>>> 'Python'[1:]  # only start
'ython'
>>> 'Python'[:4]  # only stop
'Pyth'
>>> 'Python'[1:-1] # start & negative stop
'ytho'
>>> 'Python'[::2]  # only step
'Pto'
```

In general, the step must match the direction of stop - start. For example, 'Python'[4:2] will return the empty string, which is what you'll expect in this teaser. ::-1 is a special case and will work in reverse.

If you really want to have fun with slices, check out the scientific Python packages such as numpy and pandas that take slicing to another level.[1]

Further Reading

Slicings in the Python Reference
   docs.python.org/3/reference/expressions.html#slicings

String Slicing in the Python Tutorial
   docs.python.org/3/tutorial/introduction.html#strings

slice Class
   docs.python.org/3/library/functions.html#slice

---

1.   numpy.org and pandas.pydata.org

"Extended Slices" in Python 2.3 "What's New"
docs.python.org/3/whatsnew/2.3.html#extended-slices

Scientific Python Documentation
docs.scipy.org/doc/numpy/reference/arrays.indexing.html

Not My Type

```
add.py
def add(a: int, b: int) -> int:
    return a + b

val = add('1', '2')
print(val)
```

Guess the Output

 Try to guess what the output is before moving to the next page.

This code will print: 12

Python 3 added support for type hints. But as the name suggests, they are only hints and are not enforced by the Python interpreter. The only thing Python does with these hints (sometimes called *annotations*) is to add them to the function object as the _annotations_ attribute.

```
>>> add.__annotations__
{'a': int, 'b': int, 'return': int}
```

Over time, type annotation became more powerful. You can annotate variables (e.g., answer: int = 42) and attributes. There's a dedicated typing module and more.

You might wonder why type annotation is so popular. Here are some reasons:

Correctness
There are external tools such as mypy that will check type correctness. Some teams have mypy as part of the test suite.

Documentation
Seeing a definition like def current_user(session: dict) → User:, you know what the input and output types are.

Tooling
Once a tool knows the type of objects, it can be smarter. Most IDEs (such as PyCharm) use type annotation to help with completion.

Code
Once you have annotations, you can write modules such as dataclasses.

Back to our teaser. You add 'a' and 'b', which are of type str. The + operator, defined by _add_, in str does concatenation, for example, 'a' + 'b' → 'ab'.

Further Reading

PEP-3107: Function Annotations
python.org/dev/peps/pep-3107/

typing Module
docs.python.org/3/library/typing.html

dataclasses Module for Easy Creation of Classes
docs.python.org/3/library/dataclasses.html

PEP 483: The Theory of Type Hints
python.org/dev/peps/pep-0483/

PEP 484: Type Hints
python.org/dev/peps/pep-0484/

mypy Type Checker (which works even for Python 2 code)
mypy-lang.org

Highly Valued

```
eval.py
a = eval('a = 7')
val = eval('a * 3')
print(val)
```

Guess the Output

 Try to guess what the output is before moving to the next page.

This code will raise a SyntaxError exception.

The eval built-in function takes a Python expression as a string and returns its value.

We tend to split the code into two categories:

Expressions
> An expression is something that has a value (e.g., 5 / 7, 1 < 3).

Statements
> A statement is an operation that does not have a value, mostly with side effects (e.g., a = 3, import csv).

Some languages only have expressions, and then a = 3 will have some value (usually 3). In Python we have both expressions and statements.

The built-in eval function only works with expressions, and the parameter we're passing (a = 3) is a statement.

If you want to evaluate statements, you'll need to use the built-in exec function. exec returns None, so how can you get the new variable from exec? It'll just show up:

```
>>> exec('answer = 42')
>>> answer
42
```

By default, exec will change the global symbol. You can also pass it a locals dictionary to work with if you don't want to contaminate the global namespace.

```
>>> env = {}
>>> exec('answer = 42', None, env)
>>> env
{'answer': 42}
>>> answer
Traceback (most recent call last):
  File "<stdin>", line 1, in <module>
NameError: name 'answer' is not defined
```

❶ None argument is for the global symbol table and defaults to globals

❷ answer not found in the global symbol table

eval gives you a lot of power but can be very dangerous. If you eval (or exec) a random string from a user, bad things can happen. Modules such as the built-in pickle and the external PyYaml use exec under the hood. In short, follow Agent Mulder's advice and "trust no one."

Further Reading

eval Documentation
docs.python.org/3/library/functions.html#eval

exec Documentation
docs.python.org/3/library/functions.html#exec

globals Documentation
docs.python.org/3/library/functions.html#globals

"Expressions" in the Python Documentation
docs.python.org/3/reference/expressions.html#expressions

"Simple Statements" in the Python Documentation
docs.python.org/3/reference/simple_stmts.html

Expression on Wikipedia
en.wikipedia.org/wiki/Expression_(computer_science)

Statement on Wikipedia
en.wikipedia.org/wiki/Statement_(computer_science)

Possible Use for eval and exec
github.com/tebeka/ingress

PyYAML yaml.load(input) Deprecation
github.com/yaml/pyyaml/wiki/PyYAML-yaml.load(input)-Deprecation

Warning in pickle Documentation
docs.python.org/3/library/pickle.html#restricting-globals

XKCD's Exploits of a Mom
xkcd.com/327/

Agent Mulder
en.wikipedia.org/wiki/Fox_Mulder

Index

Thank you!

How did you enjoy this book? Please let us know. Take a moment and email us at support@pragprog.com with your feedback. Tell us your story and you could win free ebooks. Please use the subject line "Book Feedback."

Ready for your next great Pragmatic Bookshelf book? Come on over to https://pragprog.com and use the coupon code BUYANOTHER2021 to save 30% on your next ebook.

Void where prohibited, restricted, or otherwise unwelcome. Do not use ebooks near water. If rash persists, see a doctor. Doesn't apply to *The Pragmatic Programmer* ebook because it's older than the Pragmatic Bookshelf itself. Side effects may include increased knowledge and skill, increased marketability, and deep satisfaction. Increase dosage regularly.

And thank you for your continued support,

The Pragmatic Bookshelf

Go Brain Teasers

This book contains 25 short programs that will challenge your understanding of Go. Like any big project, the Go developers had to make some design decisions that at times seem surprising. This book uses those quirks as a teaching opportunity. By understanding the gaps in your knowledge, you'll become better at what you do. Some of the teasers are from the author's experience shipping bugs to production, and some from others doing the same. Teasers and puzzles are fun, and learning how to solve them can teach you to avoid programming mistakes and maybe even impress your colleagues and future employers.

Miki Tebeka
(78 pages) ISBN: 9781680508994. $18.95
https://pragprog.com/book/d-gobrain

Pandas Brain Teasers

This book contains 25 short programs that will challenge your understanding of Pandas. Like any big project, the Pandas developers had to make some design decisions that at times seem surprising. This book uses those quirks as a teaching opportunity. By understanding the gaps in your knowledge, you'll become better at what you do. Some of the teasers are from the author's experience shipping bugs to production, and some from others doing the same. Teasers and puzzles are fun, and learning how to solve them can teach you to avoid programming mistakes and maybe even impress your colleagues and future employers.

Miki Tebeka
(77 pages) ISBN: 9781680509014. $18.95
https://pragprog.com/book/d-pandas

Concurrent Data Processing in Elixir

Learn different ways of writing concurrent code in Elixir and increase your application's performance, without sacrificing scalability or fault-tolerance. Most projects benefit from running background tasks and processing data concurrently, but the world of OTP and various libraries can be challenging. Which Supervisor and what strategy to use? What about GenServer? Maybe you need back-pressure, but is GenStage, Flow, or Broadway a better choice? You will learn everything you need to know to answer these questions, start building highly concurrent applications in no time, and write code that's not only fast, but also resilient to errors and easy to scale.

Svilen Gospodinov
(174 pages) ISBN: 9781680508192. $39.95
https://pragprog.com/book/sgdpelixir

Testing Elixir

Elixir offers new paradigms, and challenges you to test in unconventional ways. Start with ExUnit: almost everything you need to write tests covering all levels of detail, from unit to integration, but only if you know how to use it to the fullest—we'll show you how. Explore testing Elixir-specific challenges such as OTP-based modules, asynchronous code, Ecto-based applications, and Phoenix applications. Explore new tools like Mox for mocks and StreamData for property-based testing. Armed with this knowledge, you can create test suites that add value to your production cycle and guard you from regressions.

Andrea Leopardi and Jeffrey Matthias
(262 pages) ISBN: 9781680507829. $45.95
https://pragprog.com/book/lmelixir

Intuitive Python

Developers power their projects with Python because it emphasizes readability, ease of use, and access to a meticulously maintained set of packages and tools. The language itself continues to improve with every release: writing in Python is full of possibility. But to maintain a successful Python project, you need to know more than just the language. You need tooling and instincts to help you make the most out of what's available to you. Use this book as your guide to help you hone your skills and sculpt a Python project that can stand the test of time.

David Muller
(140 pages) ISBN: 9781680508239. $26.95
https://pragprog.com/book/dmpython

Modern CSS with Tailwind

Tailwind CSS is an exciting new CSS framework that allows you to design your site by composing simple utility classes to create complex effects. With Tailwind, you can style your text, move your items on the page, design complex page layouts, and adapt your design for devices from a phone to a wide-screen monitor. With this book, you'll learn how to use the Tailwind for its flexibility and its consistency, from the smallest detail of your typography to the entire design of your site.

Noel Rappin
(90 pages) ISBN: 9781680508185. $26.95
https://pragprog.com/book/tailwind

Help Your Boss Help You

Develop more productive habits in dealing with your
manager. As a professional in the business world, you
care about doing your job the right way. The quality
of your work matters to you, both as a professional
and as a person. The company you work for cares
about making money and your boss is evaluated on
that basis. Sometimes those goals overlap, but the
different priorities mean conflict is inevitable. Take
concrete steps to build a relationship with your manager that helps both sides succeed.

Ken Kousen
(160 pages) ISBN: 9781680508222. $26.95
https://pragprog.com/book/kkmanage

Web Development with Clojure, Third Edition

Today, developers are increasingly adopting Clojure as
a web-development platform. See for yourself what
makes Clojure so desirable as you create a series of
web apps of growing complexity, exploring the full
process of web development using a modern functional
language. This fully updated third edition reveals the
changes in the rapidly evolving Clojure ecosystem and
provides a practical, complete walkthrough of the Clojure web stack.

Dmitri Sotnikov and Scot Brown
(468 pages) ISBN: 9781680506822. $47.95
https://pragprog.com/book/dswdcloj3

Hands-on Rust

Rust is an exciting new programming language combining the power of C with memory safety, fearless concurrency, and productivity boosters—and what better way to learn than by making games. Each chapter in this book presents hands-on, practical projects ranging from "Hello, World" to building a full dungeon crawler game. With this book, you'll learn game development skills applicable to other engines, including Unity and Unreal.

Herbert Wolverson
(342 pages) ISBN: 9781680508161. $47.95
https://pragprog.com/book/hwrust

Modern Front-End Development for Rails

Improve the user experience for your Rails app with rich, engaging client-side interactions. Learn to use the Rails 6 tools and simplify the complex JavaScript ecosystem. It's easier than ever to build user interactions with Hotwire, Turbo, Stimulus, and Webpacker. You can add great front-end flair without much extra complication. Use React to build a more complex set of client-side features. Structure your code for different levels of client-side needs with these powerful options. Add to your toolkit today!

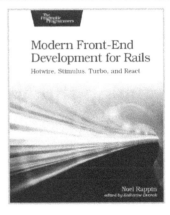

Noel Rappin
(396 pages) ISBN: 9781680507218. $45.95
https://pragprog.com/book/nrclient

The Pragmatic Bookshelf

The Pragmatic Bookshelf features books written by professional developers for professional developers. The titles continue the well-known Pragmatic Programmer style and continue to garner awards and rave reviews. As development gets more and more difficult, the Pragmatic Programmers will be there with more titles and products to help you stay on top of your game.

Visit Us Online

This Book's Home Page
https://pragprog.com/book/d-pybrain
Source code from this book, errata, and other resources. Come give us feedback, too!

Keep Up to Date
https://pragprog.com
Join our announcement mailing list (low volume) or follow us on twitter @pragprog for new titles, sales, coupons, hot tips, and more.

New and Noteworthy
https://pragprog.com/news
Check out the latest pragmatic developments, new titles and other offerings.

Save on the ebook

Save on the ebook versions of this title. Owning the paper version of this book entitles you to purchase the electronic versions at a terrific discount.

PDFs are great for carrying around on your laptop—they are hyperlinked, have color, and are fully searchable. Most titles are also available for the iPhone and iPod touch, Amazon Kindle, and other popular e-book readers.

Send a copy of your receipt to support@pragprog.com and we'll provide you with a discount coupon.

Contact Us

Online Orders:	*https://pragprog.com/catalog*
Customer Service:	*support@pragprog.com*
International Rights:	*translations@pragprog.com*
Academic Use:	*academic@pragprog.com*
Write for Us:	*http://write-for-us.pragprog.com*
Or Call:	+1 800-699-7764